The Bikeriders

The True Story of the Chicago Outlaws Motorcycle

Harper Blackwood

Copyright

This book is a work of nonfiction. Any similarity to real persons, living or dead, is coincidental and not intended by the author.

Disclaimer

"The Bikeriders: The True Story of the Chicago Outlaws Motorcycle" is a work of historical nonfiction that seeks to present a genuine and nuanced portrayal of the Chicago Outlaws Motorcycle Club through significant research, firsthand recollections, and the photography of Danny Lyon. While every effort has been made to ensure that the events and persons depicted are accurate, some names, locations, and details may have been changed or fictionalized for narrative continuity and to preserve individuals' privacy.

The book contains descriptions of activities and lifestyles that may not be appropriate for all readers. It is critical to recognize that the activities and behaviors depicted in this book are neither acceptable or encouraged. The book seeks to give a balanced and complete view on the issue without glorifying unlawful or risky behavior.

Readers should be informed that the views and opinions stated by those featured in this book do not necessarily represent those of the author, publisher, or affiliated parties. The book is intended to be educational and entertaining, not an endorsement of any particular lifestyle or activity.

By reading this book, you agree to approach the content with an open mind and understand that the author and publisher are not liable for any repercussions resulting from the interpretation or use of the information offered.

Table Of Contents

Introduction

"The Bikeriders" is a cinematic voyage into the wild and unruly world of motorcycle gangs in the 1960s, capturing the essence of rebellion, brotherhood, and the search of freedom. This video, inspired by Danny Lyon's landmark work, paints a vivid picture of a subculture that thrived on the outskirts of society, where the open road and the scream of motorbike engines defined a lifestyle.

Set in the American Midwest, "The Bikeriders" brings viewers back to a period when motorcycle clubs were more than just groups of riders; they were brotherhoods united by devotion, a shared sense of adventure, and a rejection of conventional society conventions. The film depicts the lives of many members of a fictional motorcycle club, based heavily on Lyon's real-life experiences and images from his book.

The story is told through the perspective of Kathy, a young lady whose life becomes linked with the club. Kathy, as the wife of one of the club's key members, offers a unique viewpoint on the highs and lows of club life. Her story is both a personal journey and a bigger reflection on the appeal and dangers of the biker lifestyle. Through her eyes, we see the club's transformational power, the sense of belonging it provides, and the unavoidable conflicts that come while living beyond the law.

The film's narrative structure is non-linear, blending the past and present to create a rich tapestry of memories, experiences, and emotions. Flashbacks illustrate the club's origins, fast development, and members' intimate bonds. These scenes are interlaced with present-day situations that show the long-term impact of those formative years on the protagonists.

One of the most noticeable characteristics of "The Bikeriders" is its emphasis on realism. The producers went to considerable measures to correctly depict the era, including the attire, hairstyles, motorcycles, and music. The attention to detail immerses the audience in the environment of the 1960s, making the drama feel both contemporary and timeless. The film's cinematography adds to this sense of reality, using a combination of handheld and static shots to create an intimate, documentary-like atmosphere.

The characters in "The Bikeriders" are varied and multidimensional, representing the diverse personalities that exist within any close-knit community. Johnny, the club's dynamic and brave leader, stands at the center. Johnny personifies the spirit of the outlaw biker: daring, defiant, and fiercely loyal to his brothers. His magnetism attracts people in, but it also causes tensions with competing groups and government enforcement.

Opposite Johnny is Benny, the most thoughtful and conflicted member of the club. Benny's journey is filled with inner conflict as he struggles to cope with the violent and chaotic society in which he has chosen to live. His relationship with Kathy adds another degree of difficulty, as he seeks to reconcile his feelings for her with his commitment to the club.

Kathy is an intriguing character who provides a realistic viewpoint in the middle of mayhem. Her affection for Benny and her connection with the club put her in a unique position to observe and reflect on their lives. Through her, the spectator learns about the sacrifices and compromises that come with being a member of the world.

The film does not shy away from the dark side of biker culture. Violence, crime, and the continual possibility of danger all coexist, creating a tense and unpredictable environment. These elements are counterbalanced by moments of friendship, exhilaration, and a profound sense of freedom that only the open road can offer. This dichotomy is fundamental to the film's appeal, as it depicts the highs and lows of being a biker.

The soundtrack to "The Bikeriders" is another great feature, merging classic rock and blues to capture the spirit of the 1960s. Music is vital in setting the tone and heightening the emotional impact of pivotal scenes. Iconic music from the era, mixed with a creative score, create a nostalgic yet thrilling auditory world.

"The Bikeriders" is more than just a film about motorcycles and rebellion; it's a moving examination of identity, loyalty, and the search for meaning. The characters' difficulties and achievements are universal, making their experiences relevant to anybody who has ever tried to figure out where they fit in the world. The film's values of freedom and camaraderie are timeless, appealing to both longtime motorcycle aficionados and newcomers.

The film also pays tribute to Danny Lyon's efforts and the real-life bikers he filmed. "The Bikeriders" pays tribute to their legacy while also preserving a piece of American cultural heritage. Lyon's images, which are interlaced with the film's story, give authenticity and depth, reminding viewers that these stories are based on real-life situations.

Chapter One

The Rise of Motorcycle Clubs

Motorcycle clubs have a long history, dating back to the early twentieth century, a period of fast technological developments and profound societal shifts. The rise of motorcycle clubs, particularly outlaw motorcycle clubs, reflects a distinct blend of adventure, rebellion, and companionship that has captured the imagination of many. Understanding the beginnings and evolution of these clubs is critical in the context of "The Bikeriders," as it provides insight into the film's rich backdrop and fascinating subculture.

The story begins in the aftermath of World War I, when returning troops sought the thrill and companionship they had found during the conflict. Many of these veterans found consolation and thrill in motorbikes, which symbolized speed, freedom, and a break from traditional conventions. The early 1920s saw the development of several motorcycle clubs, which were initially centered on racing and social events. These groups gave a sense of community and belonging, allowing members to share their enthusiasm for riding and their enjoyment of the open road.

As the decades passed, the culture of motorcycle clubs began to change. The Great Depression and Dust Bowl of the 1930s drove many Americans to a nomadic lifestyle, and motorbikes became an economical mode of mobility. During this time, the image of the lone rider began to emerge, along with the concept of the motorcycle as a symbol of freedom and independence. The bikers' camaraderie grew stronger, as did their feeling of community.

Following World War II, motorcycle clubs experienced a significant turning point. The war had a lasting impact on American society, and returning soldiers discovered motorbikes to be a source of adventure and excitement. This era saw the formation of the first outlaw motorcycle clubs, which were distinguished by their rejection of mainstream principles in favor of a rebellious, free-spirited lifestyle. The word "outlaw" stems from these clubs' determination to operate outside the jurisdiction of the American Motorcyclist Association (AMA), which had created a code of conduct for riders.

These clubs sought to establish its own identity, free of external regulations and society standards.

The Hollister riot of 1947 is sometimes recognized as a watershed moment in the evolution of outlaw motorcycle organizations. What started out as a tiny motorcycle rally in Hollister, California, quickly turned into a chaotic scene when an inflow of motorcycles overwhelmed the little town. The media sensationalized the event, portraying it as a violent rebellion of rogue bikers. This portrayal piqued the public's interest and cemented the image of the outlaw biker in popular culture. Although the event was significantly less dramatic than the media depicted, the Hollister riot helped to shape the outlaw motorcycle club's mythos.

Motorcycle clubs became even more entrenched in American culture during the 1950s and 1960s. During this time, several of the most notorious outlaw organizations emerged, including the Hells Angels and the Bandidos. These clubs were frequently distinguished by their severe standards of conduct, hierarchical systems, and distinctive symbols. Members of these groups took pride in their dedication to one another and their determination to live life on their terms. The motorcycles they rode were more than just tools of mobility; they were often customized to represent their personal flair and club spirit.

During this time, motorcycle club culture became linked with the countercultural movements of the day. The freewheeling atmosphere of the 1960s, characterized by a rejection of established norms and a desire for personal independence, resonated well with the motorcycle lifestyle. Films like "The Wild One" and "Easy Rider" caught this ethos, cementing the image of the renegade biker in the popular psyche. These cultural portrayals, while somewhat romanticized, emphasized the attractiveness of the wide road and the spirit of adventure that motorcycle clubs represented.

The reality of life at these clubs, however, was frequently far more complex. While the media and popular culture focused on the more dramatic parts of the outlaw motorcycle lifestyle, club members' daily lives were characterized by a strong sense of brotherhood and mutual support. Members of these clubs leaned on one another in times of need, developing bonds as deep as any familial ties. This sense of camaraderie was especially vital considering the hostile treatment they faced from mainstream culture and law enforcement.

The 1970s and 1980s saw growing attention and legal issues for outlaw motorcycle groups. Law enforcement officials became concerned about the illicit activity associated with particular clubs and began to crack down on their operations. During this time, the clubs faced multiple high-profile raids and court fights, cementing their outsider image. Despite these problems, many clubs thrived, thanks to their members' unwavering allegiance and dedication to their way of life.

Motorcycle clubs grew and evolved over time. While the essential ideas of fraternity, freedom, and rebellion persisted, many clubs sought to disassociate themselves from the negative portrayals promoted by the media. Some clubs held charitable events, performed community service, and worked to improve their public image. These projects demonstrated a desire to reconcile the old outlaw attitude with a more good societal impact.

Motorcycle clubs are becoming a global phenomenon. What began as a uniquely American subculture has expanded to other countries, each with its own set of modifications and adaptations. The emergence of social media and online groups has also changed how bikers communicate and share their interest. Modern motorcycle clubs represent a diverse range of interests and identities, from conventional outlaw organizations to clubs dedicated to certain brands, riding styles, or charity purposes.

"The Bikeriders" conveys the essence of this complex and varied history. The film's representation of the Chicago Outlaws Motorcycle Club, which was inspired by Danny Lyon's work, provides a genuine peek into the lives of these bikers. Lyon's images and conversations from the 1960s offer a glimpse into a bygone era characterized by a strong sense of independence and a rejection of conventional expectations. His documentation uncovers the humanity behind the widely misinterpreted image of the outlaw biker, highlighting their companionship, hardships, and achievements.

Understanding the origins of motorcycle clubs is critical for grasping the background and complexity of "The Bikeriders." The film investigates not just the historical and cultural relevance of these clubs, but also the personal lives of their members. It is a monument to a subculture that has had a lasting impact on American society and continues to inspire future generations of riders.

In conclusion, the rise of motorcycle clubs demonstrates the enduring appeal of freedom, adventure, and camaraderie. From their humble beginnings in the 1920s to their transformation into potent emblems of resistance in the 1960s and beyond, these clubs have had a tremendous impact on defining cultural narratives and defying societal norms. "The Bikeriders" brings this riveting history to life, providing viewers with a moving and entertaining glimpse into the world of motorcycle clubs and the people who live and breathe the biker lifestyle. Through this lens, we have a better grasp of the intricacies and paradoxes that define the outlaw biker, as well as the unyielding spirit that motivates them to keep riding no matter what.

Chapter Two

Danny Lyon: The Man Behind the Lens

Danny Lyon is a well-known figure in documentary photography and filmmaking. His art has captured the raw essence of numerous subcultures, creating a vibrant tapestry of American life that is frequently overlooked by mainstream society. One of his most famous works, "The Bikeriders," provides an intimate look inside the life of the Chicago Outlaws Motorcycle Club in the 1960s. This examination of Lyon's life and work serves as a compelling framework for comprehending the enormous influence of his recording of the biker subculture.

Danny Lyon, born in 1942 in Brooklyn, New York, grew up with a strong interest in photography and an intuitive curiosity about his surroundings. His studies at the University of Chicago provided a rich setting for his growing devotion. It was here that he began to refine his abilities, establishing the groundwork for a profession that would take him into some of America's most fascinating and frequently misunderstood neighborhoods.

Lyon's introduction to the world of the Chicago Outlaws Motorcycle Club was neither accidental nor superficial. His approach to photography was extremely immersing, motivated by a desire to comprehend and precisely depict his subjects. This manner contrasted sharply with the aloof, often voyeuristic style of other photographers at the period. Lyon believed it was critical to establish trust and true connections with the people he documented. This idea would become a defining feature of his career, distinguishing him as a storyteller with unprecedented depth of insight and empathy.

The Chicago Outlaws Motorcycle Club, established in the 1930s, had by the 1960s become one of the most notorious motorcycle gangs in the United States. The Outlaws, known for their rebellious spirit and frequently confrontational interactions with law enforcement, represented a broader cultural movement celebrating freedom and rebellion. Lyon was drawn to the Outlaws' mentality, which influenced his decision to join them. He identified them as a reflection of the socioeconomic conflicts and transitions taking place in America at the time.

Lyon's time with the Outlaws was characterized by exceptional access and intimacy. He lived beside them, joining in their everyday routines and activities. This intimate contact enabled him to capture moments of raw realism, revealing the bikers as complicated persons with their own lives, difficulties, and achievements. The ensuing body of work, published as "The Bikeriders" in 1968, demonstrates his dedication to presenting the motorcyclists' life with honesty and respect.

"The Bikeriders" is more than just a collection of photos; it's a story told via visuals and words. Lyon's images are striking for their immediacy and rawness, capturing everything from the thrill of riding on the wide road to quiet moments of meditation and companionship among the bikers. Each image has a distinct feeling of place and personality, bringing the visitor into the world of the Outlaws. The motorcyclists' voices, captured in interviews Lyon conducted while with the club, complement the visuals. These narratives add dimension to the pictures by providing context and insight into the lives of those featured.

One of the most intriguing features of Lyon's work with the Outlaws is his ability to humanize a group that is frequently maligned in society. In popular culture, motorcycle clubs were frequently depicted as lawless and aggressive, with their members reduced to caricatures of revolt and anarchy. Lyon's images counter these prejudices by portraying bikers as diverse individuals. Through his perspective, we can see the Outlaws' brotherly relationships, the personal histories that led them to the club, and the sense of identification and belonging that their lifestyle provided.

Lyon's art also reflects the greater cultural and social trends of the 1960s. The decade saw major change in America, including civil rights groups, anti-war rallies, and a developing counterculture that challenged established values and authority. The motorcycle subculture, with its emphasis on independence and nonconformity, was very much a part of this broader ethos. Lyon's images capture this background, placing the Outlaws amid a larger story of American protest and evolution.

The significance of "The Bikeriders" goes beyond its direct subject matter. Lyon's work has influenced generations of photographers and filmmakers, transforming how subcultures are documented and interpreted. His immersive technique, marked by intense contact with his subjects, has become a model for documentary practice. Furthermore, his ability to combine visual and oral storytelling has established a benchmark for narrative depth and authenticity in documentary work.

In addition to his work with the Outlaws, Lyon has documented a wide range of topics during his career. His work have featured the civil rights struggle, Texas jail inmates, and the demolition of Lower Manhattan, among others. Each of these projects is distinguished by the same dedication to immersion and empathy that characterizes "The Bikeriders." Lyon has constantly worked to spotlight the lives and experiences of individuals on the outskirts of society, giving a platform to voices that might otherwise go unheard.

Despite the range of his output, "The Bikeriders" is one of Lyon's most enduring and significant works. The book received great acclaim upon its release and has since become a documentary photography classic. Its influence is felt not only in the realm of photography, but also in the broader cultural understanding of the biker subculture. Lyon challenged existing perceptions of the Outlaws by presenting them with subtlety and humanity, paving the way for new dialogue and appreciation.

As we consider Lyon's contributions, it is critical to acknowledge the greater relevance of his work. Lyon was not just chronicling a subculture when he photographed the Chicago Outlaws; he was also exploring fundamental issues of identity, community, and freedom. His images encourage us to delve behind the surface and investigate the deeper currents that influence human behavior and social dynamics. In doing so, he made an unmistakable mark on the area of documentary photography as well as our perception of the world.

Finally, Danny Lyon's work with the Chicago Outlaws Motorcycle Club, as captured in "The Bikeriders," exemplifies his photographic skill and commitment to deep, empathic narrative. His images provide a unique and unfiltered look into a subculture that, despite its popularity, is frequently misinterpreted. Through his lens, we are allowed to perceive the Outlaws as individuals navigating their own paths in a complex and changing society, rather than simply as symbols of revolt. Lyon's legacy is one of insight, sincerity, and a deep regard for his subjects' lives and tales, making "The Bikeriders" a timeless and compelling piece of documentary art.

Chapter Three

The Chicago Outlaws Motorcycle Club

The Chicago Outlaws Motorcycle Club, one of the oldest and most notorious motorcycle organizations in the United States, has a rich history that parallels the cultural changes of the twentieth century. The club was founded in the 1930s by a group of motorcycle enthusiasts who shared a passion for the open road and the joy of riding. This original passion for motorbikes gradually morphed into a close-knit brotherhood noted for its rebellious spirit, disregard of society norms, and, at times, a proclivity for crime.

The Chicago Outlaws' early years were defined by a spirit of adventure and camaraderie. The members, sometimes known as "bikers," were brought together by a shared desire to escape the boredom of everyday life. They found freedom in the wind blowing past them as they drove their motorcycles through the American terrain. This period was defined by a relatively naive pursuit of joy and unity, as these men and women made relationships that would endure their entire lives.

As the 1950s arrived, the culture around motorcycle clubs began to change. The post-World War II era saw enormous changes in American society, including a developing counterculture that challenged authority and embraced new forms of self-expression. The Chicago Outlaws, like many other motorcycle organizations at the time, started to take a more rebellious position. This shift was spurred by a mixture of societal despair and the impact of popular media, which frequently portrayed bikers as criminals living on the outskirts of society.

The 1960s were a pivotal decade for the Chicago Outlaws. The club saw significant expansion, both in terms of membership and reputation. This era saw the rise of the "one-percenter" mentality, a term coined by the American Motorcyclist Association (AMA), which claimed that 99% of motorcyclists were law-abiding citizens, indicating that the remaining 1% were outlaws. Embracing this title, the Chicago Outlaws began to construct an image that distinguished them from normal culture.

The members of the Chicago Outlaws established a particular style that became iconic with the biker community. Leather jackets emblazoned with the club's symbol, thick boots, and an overall air of defiance became their signature. Their motorcycles, which were frequently customized to reflect personal preferences and the club's identity, were extensions of their personality. These devices were more than just cars; they represented freedom and insurrection.

Life in the Chicago Outlaws Motorcycle Club was governed by a stringent code of conduct. Loyalty, respect, and brotherhood were the foundations of their philosophy. New members, or "prospects," had to go through a rigorous initiation process to prove their dedication to the group. This process entailed carrying out numerous tasks for full-fledged members, proving their commitment, and displaying their capacity to bear the obligations that came with being an Outlaw.

The bonds developed in the club were unshakable. Members referred to each other as "brothers" and went to tremendous efforts to help one another. This sense of camaraderie was critical, especially considering the continual monitoring and pressure from law police and other organizations. The Chicago Outlaws saw themselves as a family, and this closeness provided strength during difficult times.

The Chicago Outlaws' relationship with law enforcement was tense. The club's actions, which frequently crossed the line of legality, caught the notice of the authorities. Law enforcement authorities perceived the Outlaws as a disruptive force, which resulted in numerous clashes. These battles were not only violent, but also ideological, as the Outlaws opposed what they saw as an intrusion of government power into their personal lives.

The Chicago Outlaws' environment was fraught with violence. Rivalries between motorcycle clubs frequently evolved into full-fledged battles. These battles were fought for land, prestige, and honor. The Outlaws' willingness to defend their territory and brethren at whatever cost contributed to their deadly reputation. While violence was not central to their identity, it was an inevitable part of their existence in a world where respect and authority were hard earned and passionately guarded.

Despite their gruff exterior, the Chicago Outlaws shared a strong sense of devotion and honor. They followed an internal moral code, which guided their acts and interactions. This code was built on the ideals of respecting one's fellow members, standing up for what they believed in, and upholding the club's integrity. Outsiders frequently misread this sense of honor, focusing only on the surface-level rebellion and missing the underlying principles that united the Outlaws.

The media became increasingly interested in motorcycle clubs during the 1960s and 1970s. Bikers were portrayed in films, books, and news reports as the ideal rebels, living by their own rules and shunning conventional culture. The Chicago Outlaws, with their rich history and distinct style, were frequently at the heart of these stories. This media portrayal, albeit occasionally sensationalized, helped to reinforce the biker's image as a symbol of independence and nonconformity.

Danny Lyon, a photographer and filmmaker who integrated himself with the Chicago Outlaws, made one of the most significant contributions to the public's awareness of the team. Lyon's work, particularly his book "The Bikeriders," offered an honest view of the Outlaws' existence. Through his lens, the world saw not only the violence and rebellion, but also the camaraderie, personal stories, and human faces beneath the leather jackets and booming motors.

Lyon's images depicted ordinary life at the club. He captured the gatherings, rides, and personal connections that marked the Outlaws' existence. His art exposed the complexity and inconsistencies of the biker lifestyle, revealing that beyond the rugged façade were people with goals, difficulties, and a strong sense of camaraderie. This complex representation contradicted the one-dimensional picture of bikers while emphasizing the multifaceted aspect of their identity.

The legacy of the Chicago Outlaws Motorcycle Club goes beyond their immediate actions and influence. They were part of a larger cultural movement that challenged the existing quo and sought new modes of self-expression. The Outlaws embodied the rebellious spirit that defined much of 1960s counterculture. They were both a product of their day and a force that influenced the cultural landscape.

The Chicago Outlaws evolved over the course of several decades. The group grew in importance and adapted to shifting society conventions while upholding its essential beliefs of loyalty, fraternity, and disobedience of conventional authority. The difficulties they encountered, both within and beyond the group, only served to fortify their commitment and enhance their sense of self.

In modern times, the Chicago Outlaws continue to represent the continuing attractiveness of the biker culture. Their history demonstrates the power of community and the human longing for liberty and self-determination. While the world around them has shifted tremendously, the core of being an Outlaw has stayed consistent. The club's tale is about more than simply motorbikes and rebellion; it's about fraternity, the search for originality, and the unwavering pursuit of a life lived on one's own terms.

The Chicago Outlaws Motorcycle Club, as shown in "The Bikeriders," provides a glimpse into a world that is frequently misunderstood but always fascinating. Their path from motorcycle enthusiasts to cultural icons captures the highs and lows of the human experience. It is a tale of adventure, strife, and resilience, bound together by a shared love of the wide road and unbreakable bonds of brotherhood. Through the perspective of history and the art of storytelling, the Chicago Outlaws' legacy lives on, encouraging new generations to embrace the spirit of freedom and rebellion.

Chapter Four

Life Inside the Outlaws

The essence of life at the Chicago Outlaws Motorcycle Club, as represented in "The Bikeriders," depicts a distinct blend of friendship, rebellion, and a rigid code of behavior that defined the club's culture. Danny Lyon's intimate experience with the Outlaws, captured through heartbreaking photography and enlightening interviews, uncovers a subculture that lived on society's outskirts, where loyalty and fraternity reigned supreme.

Living as an outlaw was not for the faint of heart. It necessitated a level of dedication and comprehension of the club's unwritten rules, which dominated every element of a member's existence. These guys, generally portrayed as wild rebels, followed a strict code that prioritized loyalty above all else. This code was more than a collection of instructions; it was the foundation of their existence, a sacred trust that held them together.

New members, or prospects, were subjected to severe examinations to demonstrate their allegiance and dedication. The initiation ceremony was both a rite of passage and a demonstration of unwavering loyalty to the club. Prospects were required to do less attractive responsibilities, such as motorcycle maintenance and club event planning. This time of probation was critical because it allowed existing members to assess the prospect's character, resilience, and commitment to the club's beliefs.

Once completely patched, an Outlaw was entitled to wear the club's distinctive colors and logo, a badge of distinction that came with great pride and responsibility. This emblem was more than simply a symbol; it was a kind of identification that indicated their position within the brotherhood. Leather jackets emblazoned with the Outlaws' symbol became an essential part of their identity, worn with a sense of belonging and rebellion.

Daily life at the club was a combination of routine and spontaneity, with the banal intermingled with the spectacular. The Outlaws' headquarters, also known as the clubhouse, functioned as the center of their activities. It was a place where members could relax, organize rides, and strategize about club business. The clubhouse was a bastion of trust, where outsiders were rarely admitted and members could speak freely without fear of being judged or punished.

The relationships created within the group were similar to those of a family. Members rely on one another to provide emotional and practical assistance. This attitude of fraternity went beyond the club's activities. The Outlaws demonstrated solidarity, whether they were lending a helping hand during a personal crisis or standing together in the face of external dangers. This unrelenting support system demonstrated the depth of their allegiance, which was passionately preserved and revered.

Motorcycle runs, or group rides, were an important part of their lifestyle. These runs were about more than just the joy of riding; they were about camaraderie and the shared sensation of freedom on open roads. The sound of the motors, the feel of the wind, and the sight of a line of motorbikes riding in tandem instilled a strong sense of belonging. These rides strengthened their bond, providing a sense of independence that was often lacking in their daily lives.

However, life inside the Outlaws wasn't without its hardships. The club's prominence frequently brought them into conflict with the police and rival gangs. These confrontations were a brutal part of their existence, forcing members to be continuously watchful and ready for anything.

The club's reputation for violence and disobedience of authorities served as both a shield and a target for constant investigation. Members realized that their activities reflected on the club, and any infraction could result in harsh consequences.

The internal dynamics of the club were very intricate. Leadership was critical to keeping order and unity. Club presidents and officers were chosen for their ability to lead, settle disagreements, and represent the club's interests. These leaders carried the heavy duty of sustaining the club's beliefs while negotiating the delicate balance of power within the outlaw society. Decisions were made collaboratively at club meetings, with each member having a say. These meetings were democratic in nature, yet any decision taken was expected to be supported by everyone.

Personal interactions in the club can be intense and complicated. The line between brotherhood and rivalry was thin, and internal confrontations, while uncommon, might flare up rapidly. Resolving these disagreements necessitated a thorough understanding of the club's culture and a dedication to maintaining unity. Despite these obstacles, the strength of their friendship frequently triumphed, confirming their dedication and commitment to one another.

Danny Lyon's portrayal of the Outlaws in "The Bikeriders" provides a comprehensive understanding of this complex subculture. His images depict moments of vulnerability, joy, and rebellion, offering a glimpse into the daily life of these bikers. Images of members gathered around a fire, working on their bikes, or simply enjoying a joke demonstrate a strong sense of community and solidarity. Lyon's art highlights the humanity of the Outlaws, addressing common assumptions and prejudices about them.

Lyon's perspective captures the dichotomy of the Outlaws' tough demeanor and the sensitive moments that define their existence. His interviews dive into the members' personal experiences, revealing their motivations, concerns, and hopes. These stories share a common theme of wanting independence, identity, and belonging, wants that extend beyond the motorcycle club.

The attractiveness of the outlaw motorcycle lifestyle, as represented in "The Bikeriders," stems from their rejection of traditional standards and embrace of uniqueness. The Outlaws embodied an alluring and divisive attitude of defiance. Their devotion to one another and their unwavering pursuit of freedom on the open road continue to inspire and captivate.

Finally, life inside the Chicago Outlaws Motorcycle Club, as depicted in "The Bikeriders," exemplifies the strength of devotion, camaraderie, and the pursuit of freedom. Danny Lyon's documentation offers an honest and engaging look into this subculture, highlighting the complexity and paradoxes that constitute the Outlaws. Their narrative is one of tenacity, solidarity, and unflinching dedication to a way of life that, despite its difficulties, provided a deep feeling of purpose and belonging.

Chapter Five

The Biker Lifestyle

The motorcycle lifestyle, immortalized in Danny Lyon's book "The Bikeriders," is a vibrant tapestry made from strands of liberty, revolt, and fraternity. This lifestyle is distinguished by its distinct conventions, unspoken codes, and the unwavering spirit of those who embrace it. Lyon's photographs provide a real view into the life of these motorcyclists, capturing the essence of their culture and the appeal that lured so many to the open road.

The motorcycle is central to the biker culture, serving as a symbol of independence and adventure. These devices are not just modes of transportation; they are extensions of the users' personalities. Customizing motorcycles is a highly personal experience that reflects the rider's personality, ideals, and artistic flair. The process of modification can range from changing the bike's appearance to improving its performance, and it is frequently a joint endeavor within the club. Members exchange skills, tools, and expertise, which strengthens brotherly relationships via collaborative work and mutual support.

Riding a motorbike, particularly in the context of a club, provides an unprecedented sense of freedom. The wide road, with its limitless possibilities and ever-changing scenery, provides a literal and symbolic escape from the confines of traditional civilization. For many motorcyclists, riding is a meditative activity, allowing them to clear their minds and connect with the present moment. The scream of the engine, the rush of wind, and the rhythmic hum of tires on asphalt combine to produce a sensory symphony that adds to the excitement of the voyage.

The biker lifestyle is also distinguished by its unique style and attire, which have become iconic emblems of rebellion and nonconformity. Leather jackets, embellished with club patches and personal insignia, are more than just functional items; they are badges of honor. These jackets depict stories of adventures, fights, and the rider's progress through the club. Denim, bandanas, and rugged boots complete the style, giving it a frightening yet alluring appearance. This distinctive look has been glorified in popular culture, adding to the mystery of the motorcycle lifestyle.

Under the tough exterior, the biker lifestyle is supported by a strong sense of community and brotherhood. Clubs serve as surrogate families, offering support, friendship, and a sense of community. This tie is formed by shared experiences, loyalty, and the unspoken agreement that members would always look out for one another. Club members frequently refer to one another as brothers, and this phrase is not used lightly. The group has a strong sense of kinship, which is based on mutual respect and trust.

Rituals and customs are essential for strengthening the club's relationships. These might include everything from initiation ceremonies for new members to memorial rides for departed colleagues. These rituals foster a feeling of continuity and shared history, bringing members together across generations. They also help to reaffirm the club's principles and codes, ensuring that the spirit of brotherhood and loyalty is passed down and perpetuated.

The motorbike lifestyle is not without its problems and risks. Motorcycle clubs' rebellious nature frequently leads to conflicts with law authorities and other organizations. These conflicts can be violent as well as legally precarious, increasing to the risk of living the lifestyle. However, for many motorcyclists, the hurdles are part of the appeal. The danger and unlawful status heighten the excitement and sense of living on the edge, making it an appealing option for people who feel stifled by normal conventions.

Despite the external tensions, the club's internal culture emphasizes strict adherence to a code of conduct. This code focuses on loyalty, respect, and honor. Members are expected to protect the club's reputation and provide unwavering support to their brothers. Violation of this code may result in serious repercussions, including expulsion from the club. This tight commitment to the rule ensures that the club remains united and members can rely on one another without hesitation.

The biker lifestyle, as depicted in "The Bikeriders," is also strongly linked to the physical and mental environments that the riders traverse. The open road is a place to explore not only new places, but also oneself. Long rides provide opportunities for contemplation, allowing cyclists to consider their lives, choices, and place in the world. The changing scenery represents life's twists, turns, and unexpected hurdles.

The social side of motorcycle culture is as significant. Clubs frequently organize rallies, events, and rides that bring together bikers from different areas. These events provide an opportunity to celebrate their shared passion, exchange tales, and deepen the links of the greater biker community. These gatherings are distinguished by a spirit of brotherhood and unity, as well as a celebration of the biker identity.

In addition to their social and cultural value, these events are frequently used as forums for philanthropic initiatives. Many clubs organize fundraising rides and community service, proving that the biker lifestyle includes a desire to give back. These acts of generosity defy the bad perceptions that typically surround biker clubs, demonstrating the positive impact they can have on their communities.

The allure of the motorcycle lifestyle persists, grabbing the imagination of people seeking independence and adventure. It represents a rejection of societal restraints in favor of uniqueness. For those who embrace it, the motorcycle lifestyle provides a sense of purpose and belonging that is difficult to replicate elsewhere. The sense of brotherhood, the excitement of the open road, and the ability to express oneself through one's motorcycle and attire all contribute to a thrilling and profoundly meaningful way of life.

"The Bikeriders" provides an uncensored view of this world, painting a nuanced portrait of motorcyclists who follow their own laws. Danny Lyon's images and anecdotes capture the essence of the biker lifestyle, showcasing the humanity hidden beneath the harsh exterior. His work questions the simplistic and frequently unfavorable perceptions of motorcyclists, emphasizing the intricacies and ambiguities of their existence.

The motorcycle culture, which combines freedom, rebellion, and fraternity, continues to captivate and inspire. It serves as a reminder that there is beauty in the unexpected, and that true freedom comes from living authentically. For the motorcyclists in "The Bikeriders," the road is more than just a way to go; it represents their journey, difficulties, and victories. Lyon's vision allows us to experience this journey and grasp the spirit of the riders who call the wide road home.

Chapter Six

Conflict and Confrontation

The Chicago Outlaws Motorcycle Club, one of the most notorious biker gangs in American history, was known for its staunch independence, rugged individuality, and unwavering allegiance to its members. The 1960s were a turbulent time for the Outlaws, as they negotiated a period of sociopolitical change and a countercultural movement that intrigued and scared mainstream America. Their story revolves around the battles and confrontations that defined their life, shaped their identity, and solidified their reputation.

The Outlaws' name implied insurrection and disobedience, and their acts frequently lived up to that reputation. Conflict with law enforcement was nearly unavoidable given their lifestyle and the public's opinion of them. The club's members adhered to a code of conduct that stressed allegiance to the club over all else, frequently contradicting cultural conventions and legal limitations. They considered themselves as modern-day outlaws, following their own rules and constantly defying the authority of the state.

One of the most significant parts of their encounters with law enforcement was the continuous harassment and surveillance they faced. Police saw the Outlaws as more than simply a nuisance; they were a real criminal menace. Raids on clubhouses, random stops, and searches of their motorcycles and personal belongings became common. For the Outlaws, these activities were a clear violation of their freedom and an insult to their way of life. They reacted with defiance, frequently exacerbating tensions via acts of resistance and revenge.

The conflicts extended beyond skirmishes with police. The Outlaws also had violent clashes with rival motorcycle clubs. Territorial issues, personal vendettas, and the desire for dominance in the biker underworld resulted in violent clashes. These rivalries were frequently motivated by a combination of pride, machismo, and the need to protect their honor. The violence could be brutal and merciless, with brawls, knife battles, and shootouts becoming nearly routine.

One infamous feud involved the Hell's Angels, another powerful and feared motorcycle gang. The Hell's Angels and the Outlaws were two of the most visible outlaw biker gangs in the country, and their rivalry was fierce. The battle for territory control, the desire to be viewed as the greatest illegal club, and personal grievances all contributed to a number of violent incidents. These conflicts were not only physical, but also highly psychological, driven by a need to assert control and maintain their separate reputations.

The media had an important part in publicizing the Outlaws' clashes with their rivals. Sensationalist reporting frequently depicted these biker gangs as symbols of chaos and lawlessness, exacerbating the public's fear and interest. This media portrayal, while frequently exaggerated, was not wholly inaccurate. The Outlaws did little to refute these myths, even relishing in and profiting from their notoriety.

Their clashes were legendary, with stories spreading throughout the biker community and beyond, contributing to the mythos of the outlaw biker.

Within the club, these disagreements helped to enhance the relationships between members. Their shared experience with external threats, whether from law enforcement or competing gangs, strengthened their commitment to one another. The spirit of fraternity was tangible; it was an integral element of their identities. Members knew that in the midst of battle, they could count on their brothers to have their back, no matter what the cost. Given the dangers of their lifestyle, this unwavering support system served as both a source of pride and a need.

The court fights that followed these clashes were another component of the Outlaws' saga. Courtrooms became another battleground where the Outlaws squared up against the state. Charges varied from petty infractions to serious criminal charges, and the Outlaws frequently used their own legal techniques to defend themselves. The legal system was viewed as another enemy that must be negotiated with skill and fortitude. Lawyers for the Outlaws had to be just as strong and unrelenting as their clients in order to safeguard their rights and freedom.

One of the most famous legal disputes was the federal government's attempt to demolish the Outlaws using the Racketeer Influenced and Corrupt Organizations (RICO) Act. The government sought to establish that the Outlaws operated as a criminal organization, participating in drug trafficking, extortion, and violent crime. The RICO charges posed a serious threat since they allowed for hefty penalties and asset seizures. The Outlaws' legal team fought hard, challenging both the facts and the interpretation of the law. The conclusion of these lawsuits had far-reaching consequences, not only for the Outlaws but for all motorcycle clubs, establishing precedents for how the law could be applied to similar organizations.

Throughout these clashes, the Outlaws took pleasure in their identity. They considered themselves as the final holdouts of a bygone period, fighting against the flow of conformity and power. Their motorcycles were more than just tools of movement; they represented freedom and rebellion. The open road signified freedom from societal restraints, a place where people might live on their own terms. This defiance served as both a strength and a weakness, recruiting new members drawn to the glamor of the criminal lifestyle while also making them permanent targets for government enforcement.

External conflicts had an impact on the club's internal dynamics as well. Leadership had to be strong and resolute, able to deal with continual external demands while maintaining club unity and morale. Leaders such as Harry "the Horse" Bowman, who became national president in the late 1970s, were critical in guiding the club through these difficult times. Their capacity to lead in the face of hardship was critical to the

Outlaws' survival and continued dominance in the biker community.

Over time, the character of these encounters changed. The Outlaws, like many other motorcycle organizations, began to adjust to the shifting terrain of police enforcement techniques and public opinion. The essential values of loyalty and fraternity remained unaltered, but the means of operation got more sophisticated. The club's leadership understood the need to be more strategic in their dealings, both criminally and publicly. This evolution demonstrated their resilience and ability to live in a continually changing environment.

Reflecting on the struggles and confrontations that have shaped the Chicago Outlaws

Motorcycle Club's history, it is apparent that these clashes were crucial to their identity. They were more than just defending territory or defying authority; they were establishing an unapologetically free and fiercely independent way of life. The Outlaws' story is one of resistance and tenacity, demonstrating the enduring appeal of the outlaw mentality. It's a story that captivates us to this day, reminding us of a time when the wide road represented ultimate freedom and the sound of a motorcycle signified independence.

Chapter Seven

Danny Lyon's Documentation

Danny Lyon's book "The Bikeriders" documents the Chicago Outlaws Motorcycle Club and is regarded as a historic achievement in photojournalism and narrative storytelling. Lyon, a trailblazing photographer, immersed himself in the harsh world of the Outlaws, shooting a raw and unedited portrait of biker culture that had never been seen before. His work is more than just photography; it is an intimate investigation of a subculture that thrived on the outskirts of society, celebrating freedom, disobedience, and brotherhood.

Lyon's voyage into the world of the Outlaws began in the mid-1960s, when motorcycle club culture was thriving in America. Lyon was drawn to the appeal of the wide road and the bikers' uncompromising spirit, so he set out to record their lives from the inside. Unlike many photographers, Lyon decided to immerse himself in the world he was recording. He joined the Chicago Outlaws, riding with them, sharing their experiences, and gaining their trust. This method enabled him to catch genuine and intimate moments that would have been impossible to capture as an outsider.

Lyon's keen eye and empathic approach are evident in the pictures in "The Bikeriders". Each image conveys a tale and reveals the motorcyclists' complex existence. The black-and-white pictures are stark and compelling, removing any romanticized preconceptions about the biker lifestyle and revealing its actual core. Lyon's subjects are frequently captured in unguarded times, whether on the road, at home, or at club meetings. These photographs evoke a sense of immediacy and presence, transporting the observer into the Outlaws' world.

One of Lyon's most notable accomplishments is his ability to convey the contradiction of the biker persona. On the one hand, bikers are portrayed as tough, fearless individuals who embrace danger and flout societal expectations. They wear leather jackets with club insignias, ride strong motorcycles, and exude rebelliousness. Lyon, on the other hand, captures the sensitivity and friendship that underpins their way of life. Images of bikers spending a quiet moment, joking together, or comforting one another demonstrate the club's strong links of friendship and loyalty.

Lyon's documentation goes beyond just pictures; he includes interviews and personal anecdotes that add context and depth to the photographs. These firsthand tales provide insight into the bikers' minds and souls, offering light on their motives, challenges, and goals. The stories are as diverse as the characters, ranging from tales of adventure and freedom to musings on adversity and grief. Lyon's storytelling humanize his protagonists, dispelling the preconceptions and misconceptions that frequently accompany biker culture.

The concept of freedom is a reoccurring topic throughout Lyon's work. Motorcycles are more than simply a source of mobility for the Outlaws; they represent an escape from the confines of traditional society. The open road represents emancipation, allowing them to assert their individuality and live by their own standards. Lyon's images evoke a sense of freedom by presenting bikers in wide-open settings, riding against large landscapes. These photos convey a sense of limitless possibility, in stark contrast to the constrained and regimented environment they desire to leave.

However, Lyon does not shy away from depicting the darker aspects of the biker lifestyle. The Outlaws are portrayed participating in activities that lead to conflict with law enforcement and competing clubs. Lyon's images of violent clashes and encounters with police emphasize the precarious nature of their lives. These images serve as a reminder that the search of freedom frequently involves considerable dangers and repercussions. Even in these moments of tension and peril, Lyon's concern for his subjects is clear. He presents their hardships without passing judgment, allowing the viewer to grasp the complexities of their life.

Lyon's work had a profound impact on public perceptions of bikers. Before "The Bikeriders," motorcycle groups were frequently portrayed in the media as dangerous outlaws who threatened societal order. Lyon's intimate and nuanced portrayal contradicted this narrative by providing a more fair and humane viewpoint. His images and accompanying tales depicted the motorcyclists as complex individuals, each with their own dreams, concerns, and affiliations. This adjustment in attitude contributed to a better understanding and respect of the biker subculture.

Lyon's work has had a long-term impact on the discipline of photojournalism, as well as affecting public perception. His immersive technique and dedication to authenticity established a new benchmark in documentary photography. Lyon was able to capture authentic interactions and emotions by immersing himself in the group he was recording. This philosophy has inspired numerous photographers to take a similar approach, valuing empathy and engagement over detached observation.

"The Bikeriders" also has an important place in the larger cultural scene. The book, with its striking imagery and fascinating storylines, has become a major work, recognized for its creative and historical significance. It functions as a time capsule, capturing a watershed moment in American history when the countercultural movements of the 1960s were in full swing. The motorcyclists, with their rebellious spirit and desire for freedom, exemplified the greater cultural transformations that occurred during this period.

Lyon's work remains popular with audiences today, decades after it was first published.

Freedom, resistance, and fraternity are eternal subjects, and his photos continue to evoke strong emotions. Modern audiences can still find meaning in the bikers' difficulties and accomplishments, as well as encouragement in their steadfast determination to live life on their own terms.

Lyon's work has recently received fresh appreciation, with exhibitions and retrospectives highlighting his contributions to documentary photography. His photographs from "The Bikeriders" are frequently cited for their artistic value and historical significance. These displays allow new generations to witness the raw power of Lyon's images and gain insight into the life of the bikers he so vividly depicts.

Lyon's commitment to his craft and subjects is clear on every page of "The Bikeriders." His ability to connect with the motorcyclists on a human level and tell their tales honestly and respectfully is what makes his work so appealing. He did more than just capture a subculture; he became a part of it, experiencing the pleasures and sufferings of the motorcyclists he photographed. This intense level of involvement is what lends his art its authenticity and emotional depth.

Finally, Danny Lyon's documentation in "The Bikeriders" is a watershed moment in photojournalism. His immersive approach, paired with his sensitive eye, produced a body of work that provides a comprehensive and nuanced portrait of biker culture. Lyon used his images and words to challenge prejudices, humanize his subjects, and capture the essence of a subculture defined by its desire for freedom and fraternity. His art is a striking monument to the bikers' enduring spirit, and it continues to inspire and appeal with audiences all around the world.

Chapter Eight

Legacy of "The Bikeriders

"The Bikeriders" is more than just a film; it's a trip into the heart of a subculture that has had a lasting impact on American society. The film captures the sense of rebellion, independence, and fraternity that typified motorcycle clubs in the 1960s. This chapter dives into "The Bikeriders'" legacy, looking at how the film and the real-life stories that inspired it shaped culture, media, and public opinion.

The enormous influence of Danny Lyon's work is where "The Bikeriders'" legacy begins. Lyon, a photographer and filmmaker, immersed himself in the Chicago Outlaws Motorcycle Club, documenting their life through a series of dramatic photos and honest interviews. His work offered an uncensored perspective on a world that was frequently misunderstood and distorted. Lyon humanized the Outlaws by chronicling their daily experiences, difficulties, and brotherhood. His images not only captured the bikers' tough exterior, but also exposed the profound relationships and feeling of identity that held them together.

One of Lyon's most significant contributions was to challenge the public's notion of bicyclists. Before "The Bikeriders," motorcycle groups were frequently depicted in the media as lawless and aggressive, perpetuating unfavorable preconceptions. Lyon's close portrayal of the Outlaws offered a more nuanced perspective, emphasizing the intricacies and paradoxes of their life. The bikers were more than just outlaws; they were people with their own histories, dreams, and battles. This shift in attitude was critical in transforming how society perceived motorcycle organizations and its members.

The film adaptation of "The Bikeriders" expanded Lyon's concept to a larger audience. The film captured the raw intensity and passion of the 1960s motorcycle scene, transporting spectators to a world of leather jackets, roaring engines, and boundless roads. The characters in the film, who were inspired by real-life Outlaws, were well-developed and realistic. Their stories struck a chord with audiences, who recognized in them echoes of their own wishes for freedom and belonging. The film's success can be due to its capacity to conjure nostalgia and adventure, bringing spectators back to a time when motorcycle clubs led a cultural revolution.

One of the most lasting effects of "The Bikeriders" is its impact on popular culture. The film and book have influenced numerous works of art, music, and literature, establishing the image of the renegade motorcyclist in the public consciousness. The bikers' trademark visual appearance, complete with leather jackets and customized motorcycles, became synonymous with countercultural cool. Musicians and artists were inspired by the aesthetics and attitudes of motorcycle culture, and they incorporated elements of it into their own works. The rebellious spirit of the bikers found expression in rock 'n' roll, fashion, and even advertising, as the image of the strong, independent biker was used to sell anything from clothing to motorcycles.

The legacy of "The Bikeriders" extends to the larger biker community. Bikers all across the world have welcomed both the film and the book, seeing their own experiences reflected in the story of the Chicago Outlaws. For many, "The Bikeriders" is more than simply entertainment; it's a celebration of their way of life. The film's themes of fraternity, loyalty, and freedom resonate well with motorcyclists, who continue to promote these ideals in their own organizations and communities. The film has become a landmark for motorcycle fans, serving as a reminder of their shared history and culture.

Beyond its cultural significance, "The Bikeriders" has had a long-lasting impact on the motorcycling business. The film's portrayal of modified motorcycles and riders' individual styles rekindled interest in motorcycle customizing. Enthusiasts were driven to customize their own bikes, producing one-of-a-kind vehicles that expressed their personalities and preferences. This approach helped to fuel the creation of the custom motorcycle sector, which continues to thrive today. Motorcycle manufacturers took note, and many introduced models that appealed to the film's popularization of individualism and self-expression.

"The Bikeriders'" legacy is further demonstrated by its lasting relevance. Decades after their premiere, the film and novel continue to enchant fresh audiences and readers. The motorcycle lifestyle's everlasting allure, with its emphasis on freedom and rebellion, speaks to fundamental human impulses. In an increasingly computerized and networked world, the image of the biker on the open road embodies a desire for simplicity and exploration. This persistent appeal ensures that "The Bikeriders" will continue to be a cultural touchstone, motivating individuals who want to break free from the confines of modern life.

In addition to its cultural and industrial impact, "The Bikeriders" had a huge influence on how motorcycle clubs are portrayed in the media. The film established a new bar for authenticity and depth in storytelling, inspiring other filmmakers to approach the world of bikers with more nuance and respect. Television dramas and films that followed frequently drew on the themes and aesthetics set by "The Bikeriders," resulting in a rich tapestry of narratives that examine the complexity of life in motorcycle clubs. This heritage of nuanced storytelling has helped to shatter preconceptions and create a more balanced perspective on bikers and their communities.

"The Bikeriders" has a distinct place in the history of documentary photography. Danny Lyon's work with the Chicago Outlaws is regarded as a key piece of documentary art, inspiring generations of photographers and filmmakers. Lyon's technique to immersing himself in the community he was filming redefined authenticity and intimacy in documentary filmmaking. His images of the Outlaws are admired for their raw honesty and emotional depth, capturing moments of triumph and vulnerability. This history of documentary quality continues to motivate artists who want to tell authentic tales with compassion and honesty.

As we consider the history of "The Bikeriders," it becomes evident that its influence extends far beyond the limitations of a single film or book. It demonstrates the power of storytelling and the ongoing allure of a subculture that has captured generations' imaginations. The film and book capture a unique era in history, offering a glimpse into a world that was both thrilling and terrifying. They have forced us to look past stereotypes and see the humanity behind the leather and chrome.

To summarize, the legacy of "The Bikeriders" is varied and far-reaching. It has altered our perception of motorcycle clubs, influenced several works of art, and left an enduring effect on popular culture and the motorcycle business. The film and book continue to captivate viewers, reminding them of the eternal charm of the wide road and the unbreakable bonds of brotherhood. As new generations learn about the Chicago Outlaws, "The Bikeriders"' history will definitely continue to inspire and enthrall, sustaining the spirit of revolt and freedom for years to come.

www.ingramcontent.com/pod-product-compliance
Ingram Content Group UK Ltd.
Pitfield, Milton Keynes, MK11 3LW, UK
UKHW021922190726
13853UKWH00002B/791

9 798330 303014